Beneath

Malari Lewis

BookLeaf Publishing

Presentation by *BookLeaf Publishing*

Web: www.bookleafpub.com

E-mail: info@bookleafpub.com

ISBN: 9789357616898

First edition 2022

For my son

ACKNOWLEDGEMENT

First off, I thank God for this opportunity. Thank you to whomever takes the time to delve into my craziness! Thank you to my husband for believing in me. Thank you to those who made this dream a reality! I never imagined my words would reach anyone. I'm so grateful!

Bask

As I sit under the sun
It shines upon
My face
And warms me to my core

It reminds my body and soul
That the cold never lasts
And gives me the
Strength I need to get through the grey

Where credit is due

Be proud of yourself
For something today

If you got yourself out of bed
I AM PROUD OF YOU.

If you took a shower
I AM PROUD OF YOU

If you folded one or two of the several loads of laundry that have been sitting g in the basket for weeks
I AM PROUD OF YOU

You did something today
You put forth effort
Even when you didn't
Have it to give
I AM PROUD OF YOU
The little things matter too
More than you know

We're grown ups now…

Someone once said
"We grow up being taught that the adults are always right and that you're not supposed to question them." "But you're the adult now and you have to learn to question other adults sometimes."
I am, I am the adult now
And I tend to forget that
I'm still learning
But one thing is for certain, we are not always
Right
We aren't perfect
We don't know everything
We've basically just been promoted
But the boss man sill has to keep an eye on us
Cause we can be pretty foolish sometimes
Being an adult isn't about always being right
It's about admitting when you're wrong
It's about being responsible for yourself
It's about identifying toxic traits and working on them
It's about admitting that we need help
Sometimes
It's about realizing that we aren't the only ones with something to contribute

Go with the flow

I love water
Yes, I need it
But it's much deeper than that
(Pun slightly intended)

It's constantly within me
All around me
Yet I still have such a Longing for it

To be near it
To be one with it
Watching as it effortlessly
Dances about

No wonder the birds
Sing and the flowers
Bloom so beautifully
They have no choice but to join in the
Merriment

I envy it
It is a force to be reckoned with
Yet a natural arbitrator
Simultaneously

It is so crucial
So symbolic
So exhilarating

This kind of love

I finally found a man that
Doesn't judge my weirdness
Nor I his
Instead we both bask in
The beauty of having someone to share it with
We complement each other
We balance each other out
We embrace each other's idiosyncrasies
And it just works

My Faves

Blue feels like rebirth
A welcomed breath of fresh air
Altered state of mind

Mint green is comfort
Warmth on a cool rainy day
A much needed hug

Dark Purple is crazy
The friend that makes you giggle
Random adventures

Simpler Times

I miss playing in the rain
And skipping everywhere
My mom french braiding
My long brown hair

Playing with Barbie's
And dancing around
Climbing trees and
Hanging upside down

I miss chocolate milk and
A snack after school
And spending summer days
Being mermaids in the pool

Playing hide and seek,
Tag and ball
And hanging posters
Up on my walls

I miss trick or treating
And playing in the snow
Catching lightning bugs
To watch them glow

Library books that
Took me to new places
And making my friends
Laugh with silly faces

Oh to be little again…

Let's talk

There isn't a "bad" time to pray
I prayed driving
Down the road this morning
I pray whenever or wherever I get
The chance
I don't save my prayers for
Meals and before bed
I just pray
I've prayed at work
In the bathroom
At the grocery store
God is listening no matter
Where I am
No matter the time
There is no right
Or wrong way to pray
We're not being graded on it
It's a heart-to-heart
With zero judgment

Love is a strong word

I don't love myself
I'm working on it though
I WANT to love myself
So I guess that's something

I don't go out of my way
To make myself feel bad
But I don't automatically shut
Down the bad thoughts either

I think that's partly because
I don't have the energy to fight them
And maybe partly because
I believe them

But I'm working on it…

It’s a wild ride

Being a mom is crazy

It’s exhausting
Exhilarating
Draining
Refreshing
Terrifying
Rewarding
All at the same time
It’s like the perfect storm of
Everything
All at once

Isn’t it funny

I used to think I
Wanted to be
A psychologist
Turns out
I just needed one
But hey, I’m
Still learning
A lot about the
Human brain
So it’s a win!

The eyes have it

The eyes
Story too angelic
For the
Ears to ever hear

A story
So significant
That the lips simply
Cannot carry

A Mandela
Of secrets
A Peak
Into the soul

What a time!

An array of color
Oversized sweaters
Cool breezes
Pumpkins

Open windows
Hot chocolate
Spooky movies
Warm baths

Refreshing walks
Fuzzy socks
Crunchy leaves
And warm blankets

It's all just so good!
Fall feels like home to my soul

Learn as you go

Ask the question
Even if you're
Afraid of what the
Answer might be

Have the
Hard conversation
Even though they
Might disagree

Take on that
Thing that you've
Been scared
To do

Chances are
You'll start the
Next chapter from
A different point of view

A need

Change is terrifying sometimes
But it's also necessary
It's unsettling
But it can be good
The world is ever changing
And from time to time
We have to evolve with it
If we aren't changing
We aren't learning
If we aren't learning
We are sitting stagnant
Stagnant in
Boredom
In ignorance
In meaningless silence

It’s the little things

Sun kissed cheeks
And dirty feet

Playing tag
And spotting clouds

Blowing bubbles
And spinning in circles

Swinging
And water balloon fights

I get to relive my childhood a little
While watching my son experience his

Important notice!

It's taken years
But I'm finally learning
How and when
To set boundaries

Im learning
That boundaries
Are healthy
And necessary

I have to
Constantly remind
Myself that boundaries
Are not something to feel guilty about

It's not a dirty word
It's not selfish
It's self preservation
It's self care

Boundaries don't mean
That you can't help someone
Or give them your time
It just means that you know when to stop
To keep some of that love for yourself.

Push through

I asked the butterfly
Why it's wings were so pretty
It said "God wanted to show you that good things don't always come easy." "That you have to go through a lot of messiness and hard change to get to the good stuff." It said "I didn't start out this beautiful, the process I had to go through made me that way."

True beauty

The sudden
Feeling of relief
When the sun engulfs your face

The soothing serenade
Of birds in the morning
And insects of an evening

The little joys of finding
A unique leaf or rock

The burst of energy that
Comes with a quick cool gust

How the trees
Perfectly demonstrate that
Change is beautiful

Mother Nature is truly fascinating

Beautifully imperfect

I say stupid things sometimes
I get confused (actually I'm most often
confused)
I act out when I'm angry, tired or hungry
I don't always know how to voice my feelings
I'd rather stay at home eating snacks, napping
and watching movies (preferably without pants)
Im needy
I'm overly sensitive
I tell stupid jokes and laugh way to hard at them
We are all imperfect in our own way
That's what makes us beautiful

The bright side

I'm a messy person
My hair
My car
My purse
My house
My brain
My clothes (no matter how hard I try there's always a stain that shows up, like that drunk relative at holiday gatherings that no one invited)

But I could be a lot worse than messy
I could be mean
I could be degrading
I could have an ugly heart
I could chew my food really loudly

Just remember, it could always be worse

Look a little closer

Sometimes you can't simply
Suck it up
Or go for a walk
And make it all better
It's not always that
You've just been a little down lately
You're not always overreacting
It's not that you're lazy

Sometimes it's a deep dark hole that
You feel you can't escape
It's barely being able to get out of bed
Or take a shower
It's knowing that there are things you could do
To help yourself feel better
But literally not having an ounce of energy to
Do them
Dishes piled up
Overflowing laundry baskets
Because you have nothing left to give
Then being angry with yourself for not doing
what needs to be done
Wanting to give up on life because you've
Convinced yourself that everyone would be
Better off without you

You cant always just "shake it off"
Sometimes you need help
And that is always ok

The hard truth

Our minds are bullies
They don't care if we've had a hard day
That's actually when they pounce
They make us believe the worst things about ourselves
And cut the good thoughts off right away

They push us to our breaking point
Make us feel crazy
They lie
And we have to stand up to them, we have to draw that line

Tune in

It's coursing through My veins
And giving my soul the power to thrive

It nudges (or kicks) me through the day either
In the present or as a memory replaying in my
Mind

It creates a concert within my body
My heart keeping the beat

My mood sometimes alters it
But oftentimes it's the other way around

Sometimes it's just there in the background
But other times it's the main event

I thoroughly enjoy how contagious it is
How it demands to be felt

How it can cause each person
To feel a contrasting emotion

How it paints a live
Picture that saunters about in my brain
Throughout the day

I can feel it deep within my bones
And I'm living for it
I will never stop needing music

What if

What if the last few sentences
You uttered were turned into a play?

Man, what a monologue that'd be

Or what if the last song you heard
Was now your life?

How well that goes depends on your taste

What if the last word or two of the book you just read is how you have to begin a speech at your best friend's wedding?

This could be interesting

My brain is filled to the brim with things like this

www.ingramcontent.com/pod-product-compliance
Lightning Source LLC
Chambersburg PA
CBHW062204160726
48282CB00027B/992
* 9 7 8 9 3 5 7 6 1 6 8 9 8 *